M. M. MASTROPIETRO

I0625379

THE WRITER'S FAITH COMPANION

A 30-DAY GUIDE TO EXPLORING GOD'S BOOK WHILE PLANNING YOURS

M. M. MASTROPIETRO

THE
WRITER'S
FAITH
COMPANION

A 30-DAY GUIDE TO
EXPLORING GOD'S BOOK
WHILE PLANNING YOURS

THE WRITER'S FAITH COMPANION: A 30-DAY GUIDE TO EXPLORING GOD'S BOOK WHILE PLANNING YOURS

For rights and permissions, please contact:
M.M. Mastropietro via email at mevia.mastropietro@gmail.com

Scripture quotations are from The ESV® Bible (The Holy Bible, English Standard Version), copyright © 2001 by Crossway, a publishing ministry of Good News Publishers. Used by permission. All rights reserved.

On quote pages, any emphasis made through bold or italics is the author's.

Book Cover and Design by M.M. Mastropietro
Skeleton and progress tracker images by Canva

ISBN: 979-8-218-43441-0

First Edition 2024

10 9 8 7 6 5 4 3 2 1

For God,
Daily am I in awe of Your greatness.

For I know the plans I have for you, declares the Lord, plans for welfare and not for evil, to give you a future and a hope. Then you will call upon me and come and pray to me, and I will hear you. You will seek me and find me, when you seek me with all your heart.

Jeremiah 29:11-13

Table of Contents

Introduction

Before We Begin

Getting Started

Characters

Planning

What's Next?

Resources   151

Additional Workbook Pages   159

Introduction

How to Use This Book

You don't have to be a Bible expert. This book and the Bible are for everyone, new and practiced Christians alike. If you're less familiar with your Bible, do an internet search for each prompt or use a Bible Concordance. Take those results and find them in your Bible. Read the surrounding verses (or the whole chapter) for context and understanding.

This isn't meant to be a hurried practice. Be ready to sit and enjoy a quiet study time. Pray for wisdom, patience, endurance, and inspiration. Pray all the time.

A quick note:

I share many verses within these pages and, based on the prompts, you may also love a verse I've already given. That's great! However, I encourage you to find a different verse. To keep our faith in mind, we need to read about our faith, not let others feed it to us.

I used a Study Bible with detailed footnotes throughout this process and it was a huge help. If you're looking for one to purchase, Crossway's ESV Study Bible listed on the copyright page is the one I have been enjoying lately.

My Story

Hello there! I'm so glad you're here. My name is Mevia. It rhymes with Maria, but I'll answer to any pronunciation. I thought I'd share a little bit about my life and my faith so you can understand who I am and why I felt called to write this workbook.

I grew up in the Lutheran Evangelical church in a small Wisconsin farm village. My mom was the Sunday School teacher until both my brother and I got confirmed—the practice of affirming our infant baptisms and becoming voting members in the church—and were no longer in Sunday School. She eventually started teaching again when our little sister was born and of Sunday School age. Though at that point, my family had moved to a different church.

Christ-centered influence can be found throughout my family tree. My uncle pastors a Christian Reformed church. My great uncle is a retired

Lutheran pastor. My grandparents led my brother and me in morning devotionals when we stayed at their house during summer vacation.

I have never doubted my faith or abandoned it, but let me tell you, I didn't understand the scope of God for a long time. Honestly, I still can't always grasp it. God is amazing. I see Him in the tiny yet perfect petals of Queen Anne's lace. Each petal meets to form a flower. Each flower forms a bigger flower. Each big flower makes the whole miraculous umbel—the official name for the shape.

God made that. Details as perfect as that weed don't happen by accident.

***

As is the case with all believers, I've been tested throughout my life. In one such instance, which is but a foggy memory now, I was tested through physical health.

I'm going to put in a quick disclaimer here. The story I'm about to share doesn't compare to the pain and suffering of people in the world right now. I am grateful for my healthy existence. As a young preteen/teen, however, I knew nothing of chronic illnesses and true suffering. I hope that doesn't detract from my testimony. It was a miracle to me.

One summer, at a family reunion for my mother's side, a few of the kids, including me, decided to play in a culvert leading down to the river in the park. Everything appeared clean, if not a bit weedy. We had fun. That night, I developed an itchy, raised rash all over my body. It came on like a thousand mosquito bites and the itch didn't subside when scratched. Fingernails digging trenches into my skin only seemed to make it worse. Creams didn't help. Nothing fixed the problem.

Then, the itch disappeared.

Until the next day. When it spread farther. The skin swelled like mosquito bites often do, though there was no differentiation from one bite to another. Whole segments of my skin were raised in protest. This wasn't mosquito bites. This was something worse. Something that came and went and came back again. A couple days of this torture turned into a span of time worth worrying over, but the timeline is unclear. I can't remember how long I had this inexplicable itching.

At one point, my mom took me to the doctor, but the rash had disappeared by the time we got there. There was nothing the doctor could say. I don't even recall the doctor having a *guess*.

Days and days of interminable itching plagued me until I finally broke down. The doctor hadn't provided a solution. Nothing we tried at home worked. My mind whirled over the mystery and the stupidity of having played in that culvert, but my brother did too and he was fine.

One morning, I stood in my room with the door closed, rubbing my arms with a fury, and I cried. My body was in the middle of another fit of itching and I couldn't take it anymore. How would I live the rest of my life like this?

I had no answers. I cried and begged God for healing. The next day, the rash disappeared. Not convinced it was gone for good, I didn't allow myself to hope it was over. But the day after, it was still gone.

And the next.

And the next.

It never came back. I had cried out to God in a bleak moment and He heard me. I had received a healing miracle. I never imagined I'd find the same fast-turnaround healing of biblical times, but I did and I'm still in awe of it. I finally turned to God for answers in my time of desperate need and He rescued me.

The Lord is righteous in all his ways
and kind in all his works;
The Lord is near to all who call on him,
to all who call on him in truth.
He fulfills the desire of those who fear him;
he also hears their cry and saves them.
The Lord preserves all who love him,
but all the wicked he will destroy.
My mouth will speak the praise of the Lord,
and let all flesh bless his holy name forever and ever.
Psalm 145:17-21

***

As the years went on, I had to choose a career path. In the early 2000s, the common choices were college, tech school, military, skilled labor, or farming. I didn't know what I wanted to do for the rest of my life—how could I?—but still I had to choose. The no-brainer for me was college. That's just what you do, right?

My mom once told me she could see me helping people one day. I couldn't see that. In my mind, "helping" meant doctor or first responder. I don't think patients would appreciate a doctor whose knees turned to Jell-O at the sight of blood. And after 9/11, I wasn't raring to join the military—even if that event had occurred seven years earlier. I was useless.

I eventually enrolled at the University of Wisconsin—Green Bay for Communications, thinking I would be a broadcast journalist. Fame seemed like a fun plan, but local fame seemed safer.

One semester of Comm classes and general education courses went by and I was losing my mind with boredom. The only bright spot was my 100-level English class. I didn't realize it, but I had always loved writing.

I had tried writing books as a kid, it just never occurred to me as a profession. Don't ask me why. I had always been a big reader. Books had to come from somewhere! I quickly traded my Comm major into a minor and took up English with a Creative Writing emphasis.

Now what was I going to do with that? In college, I didn't realize I needed help with career planning. So, I graduated early, cum laude, and soon found myself employed as a nanny, living at home with my parents. I was fine with that, really. I was still pretty shy. The nanny job gave me confidence. I was a competent caretaker since my sister was born my junior year of high school and I spent all the time I could with her.

As I nannied, I wrote stories and online dated because I clearly wasn't meeting people at work and I wasn't a party animal hanging out in the bars on the weekends, especially not in Wisconsin. The state that outdrinks them all.

In what was to be my last year as a full-time nanny, God put Thomas in my life. Thomas was persistent in his courting—long-distance, by the way—and we got engaged in spring only months after we met. By that September, we'd be married, but the months leading to that happy day didn't come without heartbreak.

***

In July, I was in Hawaii with Thomas when my mom called for a fun chat. A little while later, she called again. I thought nothing of it as I answered the phone, but the tone was vastly different.

She had found Dad on the floor in the kitchen. An ambulance was on the way. My brother, due to fly to California that day, was already at the airport. I had to call him immediately to stop him leaving. Then all I could do was wait for news. I put out a call for prayers on my Facebook page. I called Thomas at work. And I waited.

To tell you I cried and begged God for my dad's life wouldn't explain it enough. The dread in my gut was nauseating. An eternity passed and I got the call I didn't want. Dad was gone. Just like that. Two months before my wedding. Just days after a family get together where he was laughing and having a wonderful time. Just hours after his goofy face showed up on my phone sipping blended coffee through a straw.

I cried as I told Thomas. I cried as he bought me a plane ticket back home. I cried as I packed. As we drove to the airport. As I shuffled through security and sat alone at the gate, looking a mess.

Nobody said anything to me. I didn't want the attention of strangers while I was grieving, but it seems a little harsh now. Though I'm sure the airport staff are no strangers to tears. I cried for the 14-hour flight and layover to Milwaukee.

Do you know what I didn't do?

I didn't blame God. I may have asked him why, but I would never know that answer. I was too sad to be angry and it's not in my nature to be mad at God. I didn't get mad because my prayers weren't answered. I didn't deny God's existence because He didn't save my dad the way I wanted Him to. I can be sad. I can miss my dad. But my sadness doesn't change the fact God is there, holding me through it.

God has proven He's working in my life in many ways. Some of which can only be seen in hindsight. For example, my mother had a baby in her forties when both of her children were almost out of the house.

At the time my dad died, that baby was eight. I'm one hundred percent certain she was a gift to my parents. She brought them so much joy and served as a much-needed anchor to my mother when my dad passed away so suddenly. At that time, my brother and I were out of the house and living far away—I was in Hawaii, and he lived in Minnesota. With my dad gone, Mom would have been all alone in eastern Wisconsin. It wasn't until that dreadful week and the months following when we finally understood part of God's plan.

I don't like that my dad died when he did, but I said from that moment, I'd never wish he were still alive because I'd hate to take him out of Heaven. I miss him every day and I wish he could have been around for my sister, who's driving now, but that wasn't going to be, no matter how hard I begged.

Jesus knelt down and prayed, saying, "Father, if you are willing, remove this cup from me. Nevertheless, not my will, but yours, be done."
Luke 22:42

This is what faith is. I may not be an expert in theology. I may not have the books of the Bible memorized in order. I haven't even read the entire Bible—though I'm working on that right now, and after 30-plus years of church readings, I've read a good portion.

I know my God exists. I see His miracles everywhere—in my healing, in my sister, in the tiny petals of Queen Anne's Lace. I see His exquisite detail in the moss taking over the land I live on now. Microscopic details perfect in their design can only come from one Creator. None of this world exists by accident.

***

That fall after our wedding, I finally had a story idea that stuck based on a writing prompt I really wanted to explore. Something about looking up at the sky and seeing a different type of precipitation. My falling item of choice: ashes. Maybe I was in a darker place than usual creativity-wise, but that idea led to a full-blown book that took me quite a while to write, edit, and eventually query to literary agents. Four whole years. I moved twice before I finished that book!

Ultimately, querying that story didn't get me an agent and I set it aside, but I had a new idea I was itching to write. I finished writing and editing the next idea in half the time and started querying. As of 2024, I'm still querying that book after a revision or two. It has a message of love and sacrifice that I'm passionate to share, which is one way I can fulfill my mom's prediction. I can help people through story.

But there's more. I want to share the faith that has gotten me through all of the worst moments of my life. I've been able to survive because of the promises in the Bible and I firmly believe that if you're seeking something, you'll find it there. This workbook is to help you look for answers in the right place. It's practice for real life.

Why I made it for writers:

The writing community environment can be toxic. Published stories are glorifying sin in a way that makes the books acceptable to the secular market, but a Bible-believing, God-fearing Christian would rarely enjoy and only tolerate because we feel we have no other options.

For some of us starting out in the industry, we're wondering if we need to follow trends in order to get published. I'll admit for all of us, that we're naïve to think we can all be bestsellers someday if we write what everyone else says we should write, include characters everyone says we should, and hammer home the ideals and messages the general public wants to hear.

That's where we're getting it wrong. We're losing ourselves and our values to satisfy someone who doesn't know God.

Want to know what I've learned? The Bible says to stay away from people like that. We are to love our neighbors, yes, but we are to avoid those who will do us harm.

But understand this, that in the last days there will come times of difficulty. For people will be lovers of self, lovers of money, proud, arrogant, abusive, disobedient to their parents, ungrateful, unholy, heartless, unappeasable, slanderous, without self-control, brutal, not loving good, treacherous, reckless, swollen with conceit, lovers of pleasure rather than lovers of God, having the appearance of godliness, but denying its power. Avoid such people. For among them are those who creep into households and capture weak women, burdened with sins and led astray by various passions, always learning and never able to arrive at a knowledge of the truth.
2 Timothy 3:1-7

In that same chapter of 2 Timothy, we are reminded that Christians will always be persecuted, but God will rescue us "while evil people and impostors will go on from bad to worse." (2 Timothy 3:13) Why would we let ourselves be near to people who will do us harm? I think that includes to whom we are writing our books. We should be writing to the audience who understands us and the audience looking for answers.

As Christians, we are held to a higher standard. Those who know we are Christians should expect certain things from us. Throughout the entirety of the Bible, passages teach us to obey laws, to love others, to worship no other gods, to do good works in order to exhibit our faith, and not to fear for God is with us.

But someone will say, "You have faith and I have works." Show me your faith apart from your works, and I will show you my faith by my works.
James 2:18

Readers should be able to read our stories and know the kind of people we are by the words we share, by our works. Our writing should demonstrate our faith. We don't have to preach. We don't have to write Christian fiction, but our protagonists should be held to higher standards. Our themes should be educational and inspirational. Our villains should fall and our main characters should come out having learned something that will benefit them.

I personally have a hard time reading books where infidelity sets the course. I can't relate. I don't want to relate. I want my character to be someone I would be proud to know. That doesn't mean characters won't make mistakes. Of course, they will. I want them to be redeemable and repentant. I want to make sure the worldview of my story reflects God's worldview.

Woe to those who call evil good
and good evil,
who put darkness for light
and light for darkness,
who put bitter for sweet
and sweet for bitter.
Isaiah 5:20

So, what is this workbook going to do for you?

This book is going to help you use your Bible to find answers to life's questions through prompts as they pertain to planning your next writing project. It's going to get you into your Bible every day because I know I have only read a portion myself, so it's likely many of us are the same. The more we read, the more we'll understand, which will ultimately bring us the peace God promised and a desire to read even more.

This is how I want to help people. I want to help you embrace your faith, find peace, get back into your Bible so you can really know what it says, and write fearlessly with your beliefs in mind. We can change the world and inspire the masses with our stories.

All scripture is breathed out by God and profitable for teaching, for reproof, for correction, and for training in righteousness, that the man of God may be complete, equipped for every good work.
2 Timothy 3:16-17

This workbook is meant to bring your faith into focus by using the Bible daily, discovering what's written there, and letting it fill you with inspiration and assurance you can get nowhere else in the world.

I pray this workbook helps you as much as it has helped me. I never felt confident discussing my faith because I really only knew the basics. I could only quote a few verses from memory and any discussion I may have entered about faith left me feeling inadequately educated. Until now. I'm reading the Bible almost daily and growing in confidence in why I believe what I believe and what it means.

That is my hope for you. That this book will spark a desire to get into the Word and see all the amazing instructions inside. This will hopefully empower your fiction as well and inspire you to inspire others with your words.

Therefore, brothers, be all the more diligent to confirm your calling and election, for if you practice these qualities, you will never fall.
2 Peter 1:10

I know God will bless you on this journey. Please find me on Instagram @mevia_writes_and_reads or Facebook at M.M. Mastropietro, Author to share your progress with me! I can't wait to see how you grow in your faith and find your way with your stories.

Before We Begin

Day 1
Our Calling as Christians

I didn't ignore my calling to write, but I often ignore my calling as a Christian. It seems too hard or too scary or too peopley. However, I didn't realize just how deep my faith worked into my writing. I'm drawn to characters doing good for others, loving those who are different, and taking action against forces of evil. As it turns out, my calling as a writer works in tandem with my calling as a Christian. I just have to be brave enough to share both.

You're here because you are a Christian, too, and as such, you have a high calling.

Grab your Bible. Take some time to find verses that explain the calling Christians have. Oftentimes, we overlook these responsibilities because we're not typically held accountable for them. At least, not in person. God knows everything we do or don't do, so maybe it's time we give ourselves the reminder.

If you don't have a specific verse in mind or you're not sure how to find one, do an internet search for "bible verses about our calling." Choose one. Then, read it and its surrounding passages in your Bible. Write the verse here to serve as a reminder and an encouragement in your daily life.

_____

_____

_____

_____

_____

_____

_____

_____

_____

_____

_____

_____

_____

_____

_____

_____

_____

_____

_____

_____

_____

_____

_____

_____

_____

_____

_____

So, whether you eat or drink, or whatever you do,

do all to the glory of God.

Give no offense to Jews or to Greeks or to the church of God, just as I try to please everyone in everything I do, not seeking my own advantage, but that of many, that they may be saved.

---

1 Corinthians 10:31-33

Day 2
Digging into Personal History

Yesterday's verse is about doing everything for the glory of God. How are you called to work for God? What do you bring to the table that can be used in your faith life or your stories? Let's try digging into our lives.

Did you, like me, suffer loss? Sickness? How can you use that experience to both glorify God and teach others in your writing? It doesn't have to be negative things, either. What positive moments have impacted your life? Did you meet someone special or witness something amazing?

You don't have to be a motivational speaker or write your memoirs (unless you want to!). Just list some of your life experiences and lessons, both the good and the bad. Maybe they will impact your fiction. Maybe they will remind you of how far you've come. Maybe they were a testament to how God has been working in your life all along. Take the time to write a few of them down and reflect on things you've learned or truths you've deeply held. These can become themes in your work. How could you incorporate them into your story?

_____

_____

_____

_____

_____

_____

_____

_____

_____

_____

_____

_____

_____

_____

_____

_____

_____

_____

_____

_____

_____

_____

_____

_____

_____

_____

_____

_____

_____

_____

_____

_____

_____

_____

_____

_____

_____

How are you
called to work
for God?

Day 3

Using Our Talents

We are all unique and uniquely talented. I don't really have to say that. We know it. Though sometimes, we see our differences as weaknesses or embarrassments. These thoughts don't come from God. The devil wants us to fear and hide. He doesn't want us to use our gifts—especially not to bring glory to God. Our passions may not be "cool" or "valuable," but let's think for a moment about someone ignoring their talents.

What if a farmer stopped raising cows? What if a seamstress stopped threading her sewing machine? What if an entomologist never studied bugs? Or a botanist never studied plants?

There would be a lot of hungry naked people in danger of insect-borne diseases covered in poison ivy. That's what.

We hope that those with talents we find necessary for living would use those talents. So why shouldn't we use ours? Art sustains life just as much as anything.

God has given us many gifts and abilities. Grab your Bible. Look for encouragement in Scripture that tells us to use our talents. Write a verse or two here and anywhere you need the reminder to use your gift!

_____

_____

_____

_____

_____

_____

_____

_____

_____

_____

_____

_____

_____

_____

_____

_____

_____

_____

_____

_____

_____

_____

_____

_____

_____

_____

_____

_____

_____

_____

Having gifts that differ

according to the grace given to us,

let us use them:

if prophecy, in proportion to our faith; if service, in our serving; the one who teaches, in his teaching; the one who exhorts, in his exhortation; the one who contributes, in generosity; the one who leads, with zeal; the one who does acts of mercy, with cheerfulness.

Romans 12:6-8

Day 4
Show Them What You Can Do

Yesterday, you found verses of encouragement. You are more than "just a writer." The bank of knowledge you already possess is uniquely yours. Even the smallest ability is perfect story fodder. Maybe someday soon you'll write a character or two who share some of your talents. Maybe this is just the reminder you need to cherish your many gifts, see yourself for the amazing person God made you to be, and remind you that you can use these gifts for Him and others outside of your writing.

Now, take some time to list your talents. Are you a fabulous knitter? Do you weld? Make jewelry? Bake? Are you an extreme sports athlete? Don't leave anything out.

See yourself for the
amazing person God
made you to be.

Day 5

No Fear in Doing the Lord's Work

I know it can be scary to put ourselves out there as Christians in a hostile or secular environment. We're often called out as hypocrites, Bible-thumpers, prejudiced, or any other number of untrue things. Professing our faith can alienate those around us.

However, I would rather be known for my faith and avoided than discover people had no idea I was a Christian. I would rather live right by God (as imperfect as I am in this endeavor) than live "right" by the world.

Grab your Bible and find the verses that remind you not to be afraid to do the Lord's work or verses that remind us why we shouldn't live for worldly things. Let them be an encouragement every day. Don't forget to read the surrounding verses or the entire chapter for deeper understanding.

_____

_____

_____

_____

_____

_____

_____

_____

_____

_____

_____

_____

_____

_____

_____

_____

_____

_____

_____

_____

_____

_____

_____

_____

_____

_____

_____

_____

_____

_____

_____

_____

_____

_____

_____

_____

_____

So we can confidently say,
"The Lord is my helper;
I will not fear;

What can man do to me?"

_____

Hebrews 13:6

Day 6
We All Get Scared Sometimes

Hopefully, you found a little bit of encouragement in the previous Bible search. However, we're human. We're going to be fearful and worried because we forget to trust the God who sees all and knows all and has a plan for all.

Let's write out some fears we have, because stepping out as a Christian in today's society is hard—especially when it comes to voicing our faith out loud or in our fiction.

Take a look at the fears you list and evaluate them. Try to figure out why you're fearful of these things, where the fear comes from. Are your fears based on worldly expectations? I know mine tend to be. I don't want to alienate my internet friends. I want to be a part of their story and for them to be a part of mine. I want to network with others who can help me when I might need it. I want to be there for them when they need me. What if I overshare and find myself blocked? What if they reject me? What if they "cancel" me?

But what if I don't share and miss an opportunity to help someone who is looking for answers? What if I don't remind someone what they already know when they're having a bad day?

The world will not guarantee our salvation. Denying who we are, what Christ has done for us, and where our help comes from, even simply by omitting it, benefits no one. So, let's work through the fear and get to a place where we can rely on God's promises as encouragement when we're feeling weak. People will reject us, but God never will. For whom would you rather live?

Write your fears, evaluate them, and go back to your verses for encouragement as often as you need to.

_____
_____
_____
_____
_____
_____
_____
_____
_____
_____
_____
_____
_____
_____
_____
_____
_____
_____
_____
_____

The world will not guarantee our salvation. Denying who we are, what Christ has done for us, and where our help comes from, even simply by omitting it, benefits no one.

Getting
Started

A Writer's Prayer

God, please give me the
strength to endure this long
process.

Give me the words to help
and to entertain others.

Give me the wisdom to
know when to take a rest and
when to push forward in this
monumental task.

I thank you, God, for this
gift, this idea, and pray that
my words go out into the
world and do good.

In Jesus' name, Amen.

Day 7

So, You Have a Story Idea

We're about to get into the writing part of this workbook. So, let's take a quick look at your story idea. What is your premise? This is the single sentence that explains the central idea of your story. For example:

High school best friends reunite only to realize they should be a couple.

Your premise can be longer than a sentence, but usually no longer than five sentences. If your premise isn't concise, your idea is likely not clear to you yet. Don't fret. Take some time to think about it in order to narrow it down. Once you know it, write your premise here. An easy formula to start with is:

Character + Goal + Obstacle = Premise

And the Lord answered me:
"**Write the vision;**
Make it plain on tablets,
so he may run who reads it.
For still the vision awaits its appointed time;
it hastens to the end—it will not lie.
If it seems slow, wait for it;
it will surely come; it will not delay."

Habakkuk 2:2-3

Day 8
Keeping Things Off the Page

Our writing shouldn't put our faith into question. We don't need to fuel the argument that we're hypocrites by writing things promoting immoral behavior. Writing to trends in order to make money means nothing if we're leading people and ourselves to sin.

Now the question is: what do we do if we need to imply something sinful in our story?

The answer is simple: keep it off the page.

This can be done in romance as a "fade to black" love scene where the romance is implied but not explicitly shown—even between husband and wife. These scenes can simply be alluded to and never need to appear on the page. For Christians, any sexual romance other than married romance goes against what God teaches—sex is special and intended as a gift for husbands and wives.

Let marriage be held in honor among all, and let the marriage bed be undefiled, for God will judge the sexually immoral and adulterous.
Hebrews 13:4

This is a particularly sensitive subject to write and balance. Again, who are we writing for? What's the point of writing this scene? Titillating an audience does not a meaningful story make. If the implied sexual encounter is necessary to plot, it's important that consequences are also revealed when a character goes against God.

There is also the sad reality of violence, including sexual violence, and other graphic events. This is another perfect situation to write into a fade to black, but if you do feel like it needs to be on the page, ask "why" first. What's the point of making readers experience it? Is it worth inflicting harm? Because it could.

***

In Christian fiction, swear words are often prohibited, but can be written as "he swore" instead of writing the actual swear word on the page.

Let's be honest. We all swear on occasion. Or frequent occasions. It makes our characters feel authentic when they mirror our own behaviors. Swear words and exclamations have always existed. Their meanings change over time. What is rude one day may mean nothing a year later. However, there are arguments for guarding our words:

There is one whose rash words are like sword thrusts, but the tongue of the wise brings healing.
Proverbs 12:18

Whoever keeps his mouth and his tongue keeps himself out of trouble.
Proverbs 21:23

Scripture warns about swearing on God. Do not take the Lord's name in vain (the Third Commandment). Do not swear on anything; our words should be spoken and trusted as true. I'm paraphrasing from the New Testament here—James 5:12. Be thoughtful in how your characters speak and behave.

***

The Bible teaches against cursing, as in evil curses and cursing people. For those writing fantasy, this could be a tricky line to toe. As Christians, our heroes should not be cursing others. This is demonic and if it's presented in a way that's acceptable to readers, we're doing harm to our readers. The villains are likely to curse the heroes, but we have to show the truth: curses are for evil, not good.

We don't need to shy away from all these things, because they happen in real life. Readers need to see it handled in a better way. Don't highlight and glorify immoral behavior, but don't ignore its existence.

Grab your Bible. Seek verses that tell us how we should handle sin when we encounter it.

Brothers, if anyone is caught in any transgression, you who are spiritual should restore him in a spirit of gentleness. Keep watch on yourself, lest you too be tempted.

———————

Galatians 6:1

Day 9
Personal Writing Rules

Take today to decide what you will not include in your books. We can say we won't write a sex scene or swearing, but if we don't set that personal boundary for each project, maybe we will. I know I did. I wrote an *almost* sex scene between an unwed couple because I thought it would be attention grabbing for an audience. The fact that this scene did nothing for my plot didn't matter.

I took it out and I was happy I did. My main character wasn't put into a situation she wasn't ready for and the love interest maintained his image, not romanticizing something God calls sinful.

Also, if you're hoping to write in the Christian fiction market, there are things typically not allowed in books marketed to Christians. Consider that as you make your list of rules today.

Refresh your memory of the Ten Commandments for inspiration (Exodus 20) and see the book of James or any of the Epistles of the New Testament for extra guidance.

The Epistles are the 21 books of the New Testament after Acts. They are letters written by some of the apostles to churches and audiences in the time after Jesus' Resurrection, sharing His teachings and instructing the recipients how to live godly lives and change their sinful behavior.

Write your personal writing rules here and consider sharing them on social media when it comes time for you to promote your work. Your readers will appreciate knowing what they will or won't find in your books.

For I am not ashamed of the gospel, for it is the power of God for salvation to everyone who believes, to the Jew first and also to the Greek. For in it the righteousness of God is revealed from faith for faith, as it is written, "The righteous shall live by faith."

Romans 1:16-17

Day 10
Themes in the Bible, Themes in Your Book

When I first bought my ESV Study Bible last fall, I was excited to find that with each section, article, and book, there was introductory information that included key themes of the teachings in the pages. While many of these are very specific to Christianity, some of them, like the themes in Song of Solomon have more universal understanding.

One of the two themes listed in Songs states: marriage is a gift from God and should be founded on loyalty and commitment in order to flourish. Sounds like a perfect theme for a romance!

If your Study Bible lists themes, peruse through and find different themes that resonate with your story. If themes are not listed, search online.

Are these things your characters could learn within your pages? List a few biblical themes that speak to you below.

_____

_____

_____

_____

_____

_____

_____

_____

_____

_____

_____

_____

_____

_____

_____

_____

_____

_____

_____

_____

_____

_____

_____

_____

_____

_____

_____

_____

_____

_____

_____

_____

_____

_____

_____

_____

Who is this who looks down like the dawn,
Beautiful as the moon, bright as the sun,
Awesome as an army with banners?

———————————

Song of Solomon 6:10

Day 11

Know Your Genre

What genre are you writing in with this project?

Look up the industry standards including such things as average word count, tropes the audience might look forward to, and the ending the audience expects.

For instance, in romance, a happily ever after or a happy-for-now ending is a requirement. If you claim your book is romance and the couple doesn't end up together, you're going to alienate your audience. Know your genre and sub-genre and what's expected of them. This is writing "to market."

Write your genre requirements here and remind yourself of your themes, personal writing rules, and premise as they pertain to your genre. Look back on your encouraging verses for a quick pep talk as you forge ahead.

Know your genre and sub-genre and what's expected of them. This is writing "to market."

Characters

Day 12
Fruits of the Spirit

Read Galatians 5:16-26. In these verses, we can come up with a few characteristics for all the characters in our stories. From the protagonist to the antagonist and everybody in between. What if we don't know who our characters are? Why do this now? This is a jumping-off point. You're going to have to start thinking about your characters soon.

Choose a few Fruits of the Spirit your character can embody. Research and define any you don't understand clearly or seem too simple to be story-worthy. You'll find they are not simple or easy characteristics to possess.

Choose a few desires of the flesh with which your main character could struggle. You'll notice a lot of these sound pretty heavy. But dictionary definitions or Bible footnotes may make them easier to grasp. Idolatry, for example, could be a greedy desire to make money (idolizing money), forsaking faith, family, and relationships.

Choose a few new Fruits of the Spirit your character needs to develop to combat their desires of the flesh.

Do this for each main character—including any villain or antagonist. Well-rounded characters will make your story so much more interesting. This is an example of how we use the Bible to learn. We directed it towards learning about our characters, but it also led us to a better understanding of God's overall message.

Take a break after thinking about this and come back tomorrow. We'll be continuing to get to know your characters in the coming days. Taking the time away may help you solidify some of your ideas before you move on, saving you some extra work in the event you change your mind about certain details.

_____
_____
_____
_____
_____
_____
_____
_____
_____
_____
_____
_____
_____
_____
_____
_____
_____
_____
_____
_____
_____
_____
_____

But the fruit of the Spirit is *love, joy, peace, patience, kindness, goodness, faithfulness, gentleness, self-control*; against such things there is no law.

Galatians 5:22-23

Day 13
Getting to Know God's People

The only perfect human to ever walk the earth was Jesus. He was fully human and fully God. At first, I wanted this day to be about finding verses that taught us to have godly character. There are plenty. But as I worked on a rewrite, I thought it might make more sense to research a person in the Bible whom God chose to carry out a task.

My reasoning behind this? You probably feel far from godly. I know I do. Reading about godly character might not be as inspiring as I intended it to be. We'll never feel like enough. Hence the new plan.

Choose a person from the Old Testament and read one of their most prominent stories or the beginning of their relationship with God. *Why were they chosen by God? Were they perfect people?*

If you get anything from this exercise, I hope it's that you don't have to be perfect to do what God is asking of you. (Neither do your characters.)

For instance, in Genesis, Abram, now Abraham, was promised to be made father of nations and bear kings. A few verses later, he fell on his face in laughter, doubting what God had told him.

Jonah literally ran away from God.

Moses needed Aaron to speak for him.

If you need a place to start, choose from these people: Noah, Moses, Job, Jonah, David, Gideon, Rahab, Ruth, or Esther. Look them up in your Bible and get to know who they were. Why were they chosen? Were they perfect people?

_____

_____

_____

_____

_____

_____

_____

_____

_____

_____

_____

_____

_____

_____

_____

_____

_____

_____

_____

_____

_____

_____

_____

_____

Behold, my covenant is with you, and you shall be the father of a multitude of nations. No longer shall your name be called Abram, but your name shall be Abraham, for I have made you the father of a multitude of nations. I will make you exceedingly fruitful, and I will make you into nations, and kings shall come from you. And I will establish my covenant between me and you and your offspring after you throughout their generations for an everlasting covenant, to be God to you and to your offspring after you.

...Then Abraham fell on his face and laughed and said to himself, "Shall a child be born to a man who is a hundred years old? Shall Sarah, who is ninety years old, bear a child?"

Genesis 17:4-7, 17

Day 14
Getting to Know Your Characters in Detail

Today, take the time to answer a few questions for each of your main characters. There are multiple days of getting to know your characters so you don't get overwhelmed. The complete list of questions can be found at the back of this workbook under Additional Workbook Pages.

What Fruit of the Spirit (from Day 12) might your character embody?
How does he/she embody it?
What are your character's flaws and quirks?
What are his/her admirable qualities?
What does this character stand for or against?

What is going to light your character's fire?

_____

_____

_____

_____

_____

_____

_____

_____

_____

_____

_____

_____

_____

_____

_____

_____

_____

_____

_____

_____

_____

_____

_____

_____

_____

_____

_____

_____

_____

_____

_____

_____

You don't have to be perfect to do what God is asking of you. (Neither do your characters.)

Day 15

Understanding Needs and Wants

Can you differentiate between need and want? Let's test it. Need or want? Perfume, protein, silk sheets, gold earrings, a house, money, friends, Nike shoes.

There are really only four things we need on that list. If we weren't living in a capitalist society, the list would be three as we bartered and traded services. We think we need much more than we do to survive. We think we need a lot in order to live a happy life. We're placing our desires on stuff, when, in the end, we don't get to keep any of it. Our souls leave this earth when we die. And they pack light.

That's not to say we can't enjoy our time here. We can buy the things we want, but we need to do it responsibly. We need to know when to say, "no, I don't actually need this." Or "no, I can't afford to go into debt for this." We need to be discerning and generous instead. Other people might need what we have.

What are some actual needs?

Love. Health. Companionship. Faith. Hope. Rest. Nurturing. Sustenance.

In your Bible (or through an internet search), find verses that talk about human needs and wants and how God responds to them. Maybe you'll be surprised. Maybe you already know how loving a Father He is. He doesn't forget even the sparrows, and you are of more value than a sparrow.

Delight yourself in the Lord,
and he will give you
the desires of your
heart.

Psalm 37:4

Day 16
Getting to Know Your Characters' Needs and Wants

Take the time to answer the next handful of questions for each of your main characters. These are not the only questions you can ask of them. Learn as much or as little about your characters as you want before you start writing.

What are their desires/wants (what they *think* they need)?

What are their needs?

What are their unknown needs?

What will you give them as the author?

What won't you give them as the author?

What do they need to learn by the end of the story?

What will they learn about their wants and needs?

This is not the only way to get to know your characters. See my favorite writing resources at the back of this book for in-depth books on the subject of characters and planning.

Our souls leave this earth when we die. And they pack light.

Day 17
Beauty and Physical Traits

The beauty in this world is that all of us are made differently. No two people look alike. No two leaves are exactly the same. No animal. No rock. No blade of grass. God has created an amazing world filled with beauty and individuality. I could go into all the physical traits that differ among us, but you know what those are.

Grab your Bible! Look up verses about the human body, beauty, or physical traits. God made us in His image. Let's see what He has to say about the matter. Use these verses to help you brainstorm vivid characters and as an encouragement for you, your family, your mindset. God thinks you're wonderfully made. He would know.

For you formed my inward parts;
you knitted me together in my mother's womb.

I praise you, for I am fearfully and wonderfully made.

Wonderful are your works,
my soul knows it very well.

Psalm 139:13-14

Day 18

Getting to Know Your Characters' Physical Traits

What do your characters look like? Try to be inclusive of body types, skin colors, and other details you can write about confidently and with a clear conscience. Make your characters real. We are all God's children and Jesus died for all. Keep these pages of description handy while writing so you don't accidentally change your characters' looks in the middle of the story.

Gender

Eyes

Hair color and style

Body type

Distinguishable marks (scars, tattoos, freckles, etc.)

Favorite articles of clothing/style

Physical mannerisms (rubbing a chin when deep in thought, nervous jitters, etc.)

We are all God's children and
Jesus died for all.

Day 19

How to Handle
Antagonists

There are plenty of occasions in the Bible where behavior is called out and a new behavior is taught. Very commonly in the Epistles, Paul is writing to churches he has started in order to remind them of the proper behaviors of a believer by using false teachers and poor behaviors in contrast.

There will always be sin and evil in the world. Grab your Bible! Look up verses about wicked people or people who hate God (Herod and Pharoah, for example) to have a deeper understanding of what God finds fault in.

If you need a starting place for your search, check any of Paul's letters—Romans, Corinthians, Galatians, etc.— (or any letters) in the New Testament. The book of Proverbs in the Old Testament is also a great starting point.

Find some verses that exhibit the behaviors of an antagonist and write them below. You may also want to write down what Paul teaches us to do as children of God or highlight them in your own Bible as reminders for the next time you read.

_____
_____
_____
_____
_____
_____
_____
_____
_____
_____
_____
_____
_____
_____
_____
_____
_____
_____
_____
_____
_____
_____
_____
_____
_____
_____
_____
_____
_____
_____
_____
_____
_____
_____

A worthless person, a wicked man,
goes about with crooked speech,
winks with his eyes, signals with his feet,
points with his finger,
with perverted heart devises evil,
continually sowing discord;
therefore calamity will come upon him
suddenly;
in a moment he will be broken beyond
healing.

Proverbs 6:12-15

Day 20
Getting to Know Your Antagonist

If you are writing a villain in your story, the best way to make a well-rounded antagonist is to complete all the previous work you've done for your main characters from the antagonist's point of view.

Remember, villains don't necessarily *think* they're villains. They are simply people who have opposing views of what the main character knows is right, going against one or many of God's truths or commandments. The villain thinks they are right. They are the hero of their own story.

God made each of us as stories that hold the truth of right and wrong. If humans know what truth is, even non-Christians recognize it whether they want to or not. It is possible they'll accept reality as dictated in Scripture easier coming from fiction, which is why taking care to illuminate God's truths through your hero and villain is important.

For example, everyone knows Darth Vader is evil and there are plenty of other popular villains breaking God's Word. How do they go against God's truth? What makes them evil? Why do we know these villains are bad?

Darth Vader kills the Jedi, chokes his subordinates, destroys civilizations, and rules with fear tactics to acquire power he doesn't deserve.

Take the time to answer the same questions from days 14, 16, and 18 using the character question worksheet provided in the back of the workbook. Your antagonist will probably not appear on the page nearly as often as your hero, but understanding your villain will make each appearance more impactful.

Taking care to illuminate God's truths through your hero and villain is important.

_____

Day 21
Conflict Outside of Villains

God calls us to be sanctified, which means to be set apart by God and for God, for sacred, holy purposes. But we are not fully sanctified the minute we accept Jesus. It's a process. We grow as we learn more about God and Jesus. In this learning, we often come up against hard things. To make your writing authentic, your main character will need to experience conflict unrelated to the villain.

This could be anything. House fires, death, disagreements, sickness, injury, loneliness, temptations. There is conflict at every turn. It's how we view this conflict that helps us to grow in our faith. We should view it as a trial being allowed by God. He didn't cause it, but He let us meet it. Therefore, in these trials, we are learning and growing spiritually.

Grab your Bible! Look up verses about dealing with conflict. How does God want us to continue when life gets hard? Remember, if you're not sure where to look in the Bible, that's okay! Do a quick internet search to find relevant verses, then go read them and the surrounding chapter in your Bible.

_____

_____

_____

_____

_____

_____

_____

_____

_____

_____

_____

_____

_____

_____

_____

_____

_____

_____

_____

_____

_____

_____

_____

_____

_____

_____

_____

_____

_____

_____

_____

_____

_____

_____

_____

_____

Put on then, as *God's chosen ones*, holy and beloved, compassionate hearts, kindness, humility, meekness, and patience, bearing with one another and, if one has a complaint against another, forgiving each other, as the Lord has forgiven you, so you also must forgive.

Colossians 3:12-13

Day 22
If Not a Villain...

Oftentimes characters are not fighting an evil sorcerer or escaping a kidnapper, but rather dealing with unexpected, tragic, or even annoying situations. If your main plot is not about a conflict with a villain, work that out here. Sometimes a story will have a villain *and* a situation causing conflict for the main character. Consider that as well.

> If not a person, what is your main character up against?
> What situation is harming your main character?
> What will it teach them?

There is conflict at every turn. It's how we view this conflict that helps us to grow in our faith.

Planning

Day 23
Belonging

Oftentimes we feel like we don't belong in the time period we're living in. Or we wish we lived in a different country or had a bigger house or owned a larger property outside a sprawling city. We aren't content with where we are in life, even if only in the physical, geographical sense. We feel like we don't belong and can't reconcile that feeling.

But we were put where (and when) we are for a reason. Our setting is a part of our story and maybe we were born "for such a time as this." (Esther 4:14)

Grab your Bible! What encouragement can you find about belonging?

And he made from one man every nation of mankind to live on all the face of the earth, having determined allotted periods and the boundaries of their dwelling place, that they should seek God, and perhaps feel their way toward him and find him.

Yet he is actually not far from each one of us.

Acts 17:26-27

Day 24
Where Your Characters Belong

Now think about your story setting. A good setting can often be described as its own character.

Where does your story take place?

Is there more than one location?

What do these places look like?

What do you hope your setting will make readers feel? (Knowing this going in will help you write vivid scenes to invoke these feelings.)

What can readers and characters alike learn from your setting, if anything?

Will your setting hold any clues to what happens later in the story?

How is your character dissatisfied with this setting? Or are they?

Our setting is a part of our story and maybe we were born "for such a time as this."

Day 25
Plots and Prophecies

Grab your Bible! There is an entire section of Prophetic Books in the Old Testament that teaches us what was happening in the times of the prophets as well as what God was orchestrating for the future, including the fall of powerful kingdoms, Christ's coming, Christ's crucifixion, and the final day of judgment. The book of Daniel has a prophecy that explains the changes in rulers over an extended period of time. It can be supported by other historical accounts.

Sounds like plotting to me! Jokes aside, find instances in the Old Testament that revealed what was coming in the New Testament. Or find prophecies that depict other moments in history. This serves to show how God has been working throughout history.

The prophetic books include: Isaiah, Jeremiah, Lamentations, Ezekiel, Daniel, Hosea, Joel, Amos, Obadiah, Jonah, Micah, Nahum, Habakkuk, Zephaniah, Haggai, Zechariah, and Malachi.

And again, Isaiah says,

"The root of Jesse will come,
even he who arises to rule the Gentiles;
in him will the Gentiles hope."

Romans 15:12 (Paul quoting Isaiah)

Day 26
Plotting Your Story

The Old Testament prophecies show God had a perfect plan and nothing stood in the way. This is still true today.

Maybe this is a little deep for fiction writing, but planning your story is important. You were meant to write this story.

There are arguments all over the internet about plotting versus pantsing versus "plantsing" (a combination of both). I'm going to suggest you plot your story. You have something to say. It's beneficial to plan how you're going to get from one plot point to the next in order to do your story justice.

Maybe you're more of a discovery writer. That's great! Don't take this to mean you can't make changes to your outline when your idea develops differently than you thought it would when you began writing. Your plot outline isn't a pair of handcuffs. You are free to change it at any time however you see fit.

But trust me. You need to keep track of all your important details. Every little thing that matters at the end of the book has to come from somewhere earlier in the story.

***

Plotting doesn't have to be done in pages and pages of outline when following the Plot Skeleton method. I first learned it from Dr. Angela Hunt's book, *Writing Lessons from the Front.* My cousin introduced me to this book and it got my early writing off the ground. Years later, I plotted a book scene by scene and it was tedious. The Plot Skeleton method will give you a lot of freedom in the drafting phase.

One quick thought before we begin:

What is the message you hope readers will receive by the end of your story?

Think about how to get to that outcome as you plot. If you know what that message is, write it on the lines provided.

For more in-depth story planning instruction, read *The Anatomy of Story* by John Truby. He goes into thorough detail of all aspects of a story and helps to plan down to the scene and dialogue level. I highly recommend it. His book and other resources can be found in the *My Favorite Resources* section at the end of this book.

***

Now for the plot skeleton breakdown: It is a formula, but your story won't feel formulaic. Find the skeleton worksheets at the back of this workbook or draw your own.

The Head: State one obvious need and one hidden need.

The Neck: The inciting incident.

The Ribs: The complications. The last complication leads to the bleakest moment.

Draw your skeleton with at least three ribs. Each rib has a negative moment followed by a positive moment that keeps your character going. If he/she didn't have hope, he/she would give up.

The Tailbone: The final goal.

The Thighbone: After the bleakest moment, your protagonist needs help. Someone gives him a push in the right direction.

The Knee: After considering what the helper said/did, your protagonist learns a lesson.

The Shin Bone: The character decides to act on what he's learned.

The Foot: The decision leads to the resolution. The character either meets the goal or doesn't.

There! You've plotted your story with the bare minimum information.

If you have multiple important characters in your story, you will want to fill out a plot skeleton for each character. Again, worksheets can be found at the back of the workbook or you can hand draw your own. Below is some space for taking notes as you think things through and consider your story's message to readers.

What is the message you hope readers will receive by the end of your story?

What's Next?

Day 27

Ready Yourself for Work

You have now started to plan one of the hardest things you will ever do. Millions of people say they want to write a book. Only the tiniest percent ever see it to completion. This is an endeavor. It is a slog at times and you're going to want to quit.

Don't give in.

Grab your Bible! Look for verses about readying yourself for work. Search for verses you will find encouraging on the hard days, because I guarantee there will be those days. But just because it's hard, doesn't meant it's bad. See it through.

Therefore, since we are surrounded by so great a cloud of witnesses, let us also lay aside every weight, and sin which clings so closely, and

let us run with endurance the race that is set before us,

looking to Jesus, the founder and perfecter of our faith, who for the joy that was set before him endured the cross, despising the shame, and is seated at the right hand of the throne of God.

Hebrews 12:1-2

Day 28
Make a Plan

It's almost time to start drafting. But first, take a look at your life: daily responsibilities, work, kids, nutrition, rest. How much time can you devote on a weekly basis to writing? Start thinking about when you'll be putting in the work to write, because it is work. Work with only personal satisfaction of having done it as the initial reward.

Don't go overboard thinking you're going to finish your novel in a month. You might be able to complete a first draft, but that effort is not sustainable for an entire writing career. I never personally subscribed to that agenda. I would be burned out in days trying to keep up with the daily word count needed to finish a novel in a month!

God has deemed rest to be important. Take care to avoid burnout and exhaustion in all aspects of your life, including writing.

**It is vain that you rise up early
and go late to rest,
eating the bread of anxious toil;
for he gives to his beloved sleep.
Psalm 127:2**

Decide how often you'll be able to write during the week, what time of day, and for how long. State that intention below. You'll need to hold yourself accountable. If that's going to be hard to do, tell someone close to you about your goals. Ask them to help you stay on task.

If you think a word count goal for the week will be better for you, that's okay too! Write it below. You may also want to write down the things you think might stop you from completing your daily/weekly goals and consider a backup plan. This plan is also not set in stone. You can adjust as you go.

_____
_____
_____
_____
_____
_____
_____
_____
_____
_____
_____
_____
_____
_____
_____
_____
_____
_____
_____
_____
_____

It is vain that you rise up
early
and go late to rest,
eating the bread of anxious
toil;
for he gives to his beloved
sleep.

Psalm 127:2

Day 29

Set the Mood

If you're a first-time writer, you may not know what work environment you'll prefer. Play around with it. Would you rather sit at your dining table, a desk, or on the couch? Keep in mind your posture and wrists. Nobody wants a hump and carpal tunnel.

Want some ambience? Light a candle. Find some music that doesn't distract you. Get cozy blankets. Steep some tea and grab a snack. Diffuse energizing essential oils. Bribe your dog to sit with you.

Play with your environment and switch it up once in a while to see if you're more productive elsewhere.

Maybe leaving the house works better for you. Go to the library or a coffee shop. Explore your options and have fun. Writing is going to be hard, but that doesn't mean you can't enjoy the struggle.

What worked and what didn't?

It may help to write this stuff down for future you. I tend to think I can write in front of the television. It's not true. Remind yourself what actually inhibited your progress.

_____

_____

_____

_____

_____

_____

_____

_____

_____

_____

_____

_____

_____

_____

_____

_____

_____

_____

_____

_____

_____

_____

_____

_____

_____

Writing is going to be hard, but that doesn't mean you can't enjoy the struggle.

Day 30
Ready to Roll!

Grab your Bible! Look up verses about going out into the world, because you're venturing into new territory here. There are going to be days you will need encouragement.

Keep this workbook close in order to have all the verses you've found and the details of your project close. Remember the personal rules you've written and the themes you're hoping to share. Is everything you've planned lined up to support your themes?

There's no way to explain the joy of writing and finishing a book. But in the midst of the exciting twists and turns, there will be struggle. There will be doubt. Don't let it overcome you. Come back to your inspirational verses and pray over yourself and your project often.

Keep reading Scripture. By nature, it is inspiring and encouraging. It is the greatest book ever written and you're trying to write great books, too. Write your verses about going out into the world below.

_____

_____

_____

_____

_____

_____

_____

_____

_____

_____

_____

_____

_____

_____

_____

_____

_____

_____

_____

_____

_____

_____

_____

_____

_____

_____

_____

_____

_____

_____

_____

_____

_____

_____

_____

_____

For at one time you were darkness, but now you are light in the Lord.

Walk as children of light.

Ephesians 5:8

What's Next?

It's a long haul between planning and finishing work, but you can get there. Remember the first draft is never the one that gets published. Get it done as fast as possible, perfectly imperfect, and start editing. Edits will take time.

Take note if your idea changed as you wrote it. Does it still share a message you find important? Does it still line up with your themes? Fix anything you need to and prepare to revise again and again. But don't be discouraged. This is how the process goes.

Before you edit too many drafts, however, you'll need to find the courage to let someone else read your work. Don't bother letting anyone read your first draft. That one was for you. Share draft two, three, or four with a critique partner and/or a trusted group of writers and readers. The sooner you share a draft, the sooner plot holes or other problems you may have missed can be pointed out.

Get valuable feedback and encouragement, but don't fish for compliments. Find out where your story is working and where it isn't. Then revise some more. It's also a great idea to take time away from your project. Distance gives clarity. Repeat these steps until you feel you've done all you can to make your message shine.

Look back on your encouraging Bible verses when you lose steam. Know when to take a break and for how long. This is an immense undertaking and you're doing it! Don't quit.

And we know that for those who love God

all things work together for good,

for those who are called according to his purpose.

Romans 8:28

Conclusion

We've taken this month to dig into the Bible, finding lessons and advice for all kinds of questions in life. That was the main goal. We've done it. We've increased our understanding of God's Word and purpose.

We've also planned a novel.

Now it's up to you. You can continue to read the Bible every day to understand more and find the hope God's Word provides. There is an answer for everything in the Bible and each answer is a step closer to sanctification—becoming holy—and growing closer to resembling Jesus.

My supreme desire is that you will grow desperate in your need for the Word. It is a constant comfort in my life and has formed who I am as a person. I am at peace, especially after reading the Bible and learning evil never wins. It is repeated at every turn in one way or another. Evil never wins.

The more you turn to the Bible, the greater your desire to read more of it. You only need to start. If you want a place to begin, try the book of James in the New Testament because it gives a succinct overview of what it means to be a Christian. Or pick any of the short books by checking the table of contents so you're not overwhelmed by length. Then read John. Then hop backwards to the Old Testament. Choose anything.

You will start to put together history and see how God is working throughout it.

I also recommend using a Study Bible that includes footnotes on every page. Understanding the chapter by reading the footnotes first was pivotal for me. The footnotes explained everything that was said. I also highly recommend the English Standard Version Bible translation for ease of language.

Another thing I've learned as I've been reading is that most online Christians haven't read the Bible. You can tell by their actions and their words. They're misunderstanding and misrepresenting. Part of my desire for you to read the Bible on your own is so that you know what it actually says. This is why I'm not interpreting anything. I'm sending you on the scavenger hunt for answers. God and the Holy Spirit will help you understand as you read. You only need to start.

Sound weird? Probably. But as you read, it will become clear. God wants a relationship with you and it starts by learning about Him.

Which takes us to our projects. The more we learn about God, the more we want to please Him and bring others to know Him. This is why this book is made for writers. We have the opportunity to share our faith through our words. Many Christians are writing in a way that glorifies God all the time. It's not uncommon.

Your incredible story idea can become Christian fiction, but it doesn't have to. No matter the genre, your fiction can reflect truth, honor Christ, and make an impact. It's what the characters learn by the end of the story that will impact readers forever. It's not how often they swear or have sex. The number of books you sell because your story is trendy or "spicy" isn't going to help others come to know God—which is our true purpose as Christians. Sales and income are all well and good, but are you writing something you're proud of? That God would commend you for? Does it reflect Him?

When you come before God at the end of your life and give an account of what you've done with it, will it please Him?

I hope this workbook has helped you to embrace your faith and write fearlessly with your beliefs in mind. We can change the world and inspire the masses with our stories.

I hope this workbook brought your faith into focus by using the Bible, discovering what's written there, and letting it fill you with inspiration and assurance you can get nowhere else in the world.

I hope it has inspired you to read more, to learn more, and to grow.

I hope you've realized you don't have to be perfect to do what God is asking of you.

You have done an excellent job. I'll be praying for you and your book. Find me and share your progress on Instagram @mevia_writes_and_reads or on Facebook at M.M. Mastropietro, Author.

God bless you always.
~M

Enter by the narrow gate. For the gate is wide and the way is easy that leads to destruction, and those who enter by it are many. For the gate is narrow and the way is hard that leads to life, and those who find it are few.

Matthew 7:13-14

Resources

Prayers for the Process

Dear God,
Please give me the words today. Please help me not to quit. Guide me as I write this important work and help me to find my way. Amen.

Dear God,
Today, I'm tired. Please help me not to feel guilty as I rest. Remind me that you rested, too. Don't let me get caught in the hustle, but take a break to come back refreshed and ready. Amen.

Dear God,
Remind me that You alone are perfect. My sense of worth is not dependent on the value of my words. Amen.

Dear God,
Please help me to share your truths in a way that honors You. Don't let me get so caught up in the writing that I forget the message. Amen.

Dear God,
Grant that as I grow to know You better, my effectiveness as a writer may also grow. Amen.

Dear God,
Let my work reflect the fact that I am a child of God, created in Christ Jesus. Amen.

Dear God,
Please help me to not grow weary or lazy in my writing. Help me to run with perseverance the race set before me in writing. Amen.

Dear God,
Thank you for joy and the joy of writing to please you. Amen.

My Favorite Resources

Faith

In Touch Ministries
The 30 Life Principles by Dr. Charles Stanley
The Daily Grace Co.
Liturgy of the Ordinary by Tish Harrison Warren
Knowing Scripture by R.C. Sproul

Writing

The Anatomy of Story by John Truby
The Emotional Craft of Fiction by Donald Maass
Breathing Life into Your Characters by Rachel Ballon
Writing Down the Bones by Natalie Goldberg
Writing Lessons from the Front by Dr. Angela Hunt

Christian Musicians

Lauren Daigle
Francesca Battistelli
Riley Clemmons
Chris August
Holly Starr
Anne Wilson
Christy Nockels
Dara Maclean
Carrie Underwood

Christian Market Standards

Keep in mind, specific guidelines may vary from publisher to publisher. However, most Christian fiction will follow these standards and can be found through a quick internet search:

Reflect and uphold Christian principles, such as love, forgiveness, redemption, and faith. Align with biblical teachings and promote a Christian worldview.

Avoid explicit or gratuitous language, violence, and sexual content. Aim to provide uplifting and inspiring stories that can be enjoyed by readers of all ages.

Stories often incorporate spiritual elements, such as characters' spiritual journeys, faith struggles, or the exploration of biblical truths. These themes can serve to encourage readers' spiritual growth and understanding.

Characters are usually depicted as flawed individuals seeking transformation through their faith.

Stories often emphasize the redemptive power of God's grace and the hope found in Christ. They may explore themes of forgiveness, second chances, and the transformative impact of faith on characters' lives.

Christian fiction seeks to inspire and encourage readers. Convey messages of hope, perseverance, and the power of faith, leaving readers with a sense of encouragement and a deeper connection to God.

Works Cited

Hunt, Angela. "The Plot Skeleton." Writing Lessons from the Front. Hunt Haven Press. 2014. pp. 7-29.

ESV Study Bible. Crossway. 2016.

Skeleton image and Progress Trackers from Canva

Acknowledgments

Thank you, God, for guiding me through this project and through life. What started as an idea for a downloadable, passive-income project soon became a full-fledged book, and that's because of You. At any moment of doubt, I prayed to You and You helped me remember that this book was meant for more. My fears couldn't stop it. I pray now that it finds someone who needs it and through it, they find You have always been there for them, too.

Thank you, Thomas John, for loving me and being the supportive husband I never knew I needed. I always think I can do anything. By myself. No matter how hard it is. And while I'm stubborn and know I am fully capable of doing *anything* I put my mind to (as long as *I* want to), I'm glad you're my teammate and partner who doesn't let me do life or hard things alone.

Thank you, Mom, for being the person I talk to the most and my best friend. Thank you for teaching me about my faith. Thank you for loving me and being there anytime I need you. Your generous heart is your greatest gift.

Thank you, Dad, for keeping your Bible in the bathroom so we knew you read it daily. This quiet exhibit of your faith had a lasting impression. I can't wait to hear your laugh again.

Thank you, Lydia Gappa, for being the best cousin/sister/friend a girl could ask for. Thank you for being my playmate. It was a magical day when I finally realized you loved to play with toys and use your imagination like I did. Thank you for always being a willing reader of my projects, the best alpha-reader/critique partner, and encourager of dreams. You are so special to me.

Thank you to my rock star brother, Frank Gappa, for being my first playmate and best friend. Thank you for pursuing your own creative dreams so we can be "starving artists" together.

Thank you, Clare, for being the best cheerleader for my projects and growing into your role as best friend, not only little sister. I prayed for you way before you were born because I wanted to play with a real live baby. God answered that prayer, too.

Thank you, Grandpa, for walking me down the aisle and calling me every Friday morning at nine. I love you.

Thank you, beta readers: Amber Hook, Megan Riann, Laura Detering, Ashley Kragt, and Hannah Stone. All of your notes were immensely helpful. Your excitement for using this project when planning your next stories reminded me exactly why I set out to create it. I can't wait to see what you all do next. You are all so talented and special. I'm very happy to know you.

Thank you to my wonderful Instagram writing family. I have learned so much from you and value all that you share. I can't wait to see where we all end up!

And thank *you*, reader, for giving this book a chance. I hope it was exactly what you needed.

As always, reviews help authors and readers. I'd be ever so grateful if you left a review online so others could find this book. Thank you!

About the Author

M. M. Mastropietro is a happy homebody. She reads slowly, loves cheese pizza, and doesn't understand vegetables. She lives in the Midwest with her husband and Siberian husky, Kiska.

When she's not admiring nature and homemaking, she's writing books that tackle hard truths and ugly realities in often dystopian or unusual, speculative-ish settings.

She craves found families, bodyguards, and "he falls first" tropes mixed with high stakes and suspenseful action in "us against the world" stories.

Visit her at www.mmmastropietrobooks.com for more information about future releases.

Additional Workbook Pages

Character Worksheet

Complete list of character questions:

What Fruit of the Spirit might your character embody?
How does he/she embody it?
What are your character's flaws and quirks?
What are his/her admirable qualities?
What does this character stand for or against?

What is going to light your character's fire?
What are their desires/wants (what they *think* they need)?
What are their needs?
What are their unknown needs?

What will you give them as the author?
What won't you give them as the author?
What do they need to learn by the end of the story?
What will they learn about their wants and needs?

Physical Traits
Gender
Eyes
Hair color and style
Body Type
Distinguishable marks (i.e. scars, tattoos, freckles, etc.)
Favorite articles of clothing/style
Physical mannerisms (i.e. rubbing a chin when deep in thought, nervous jitters, etc.)

My Favorite Verses

My Weekly Goals

Plotting

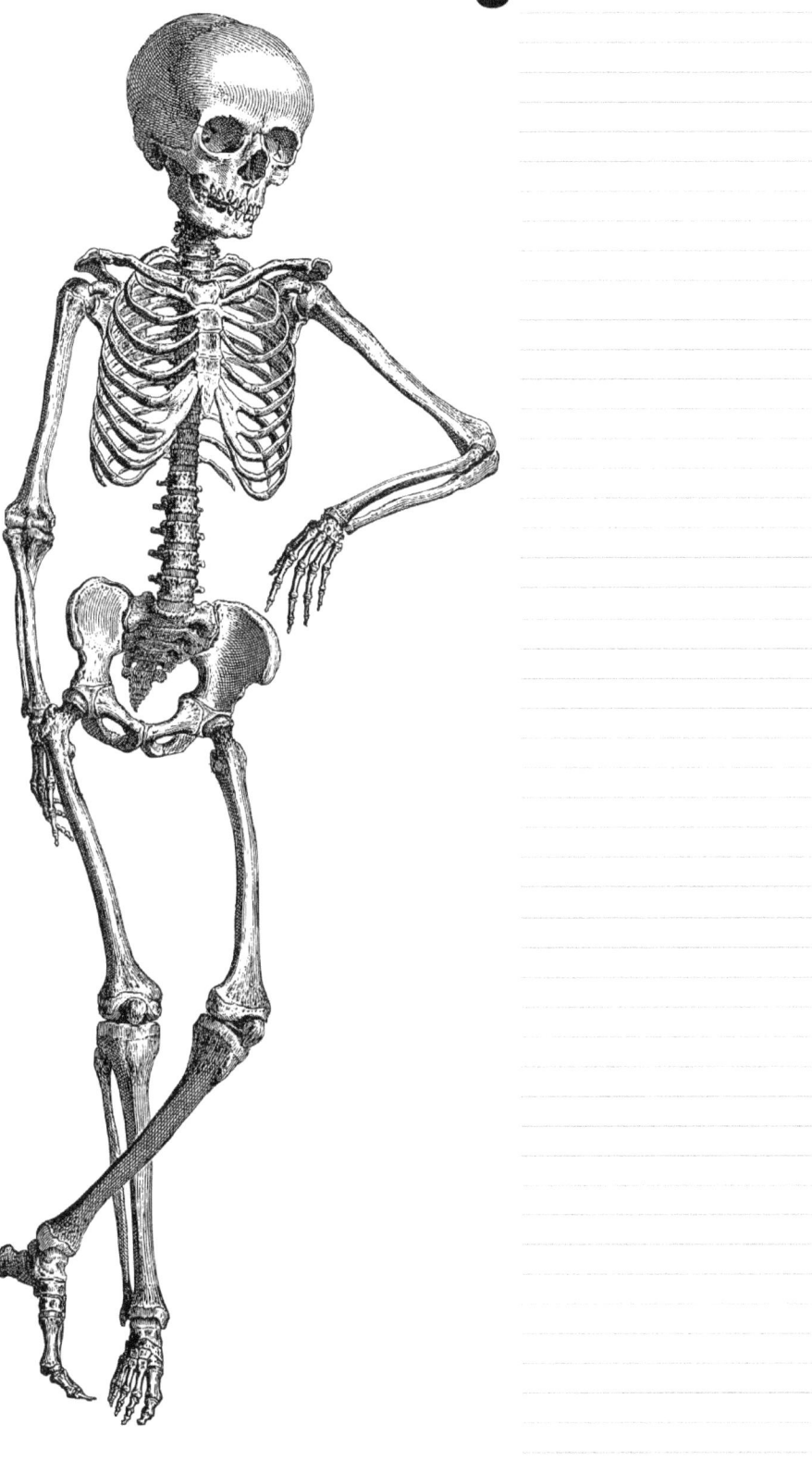

Plotting

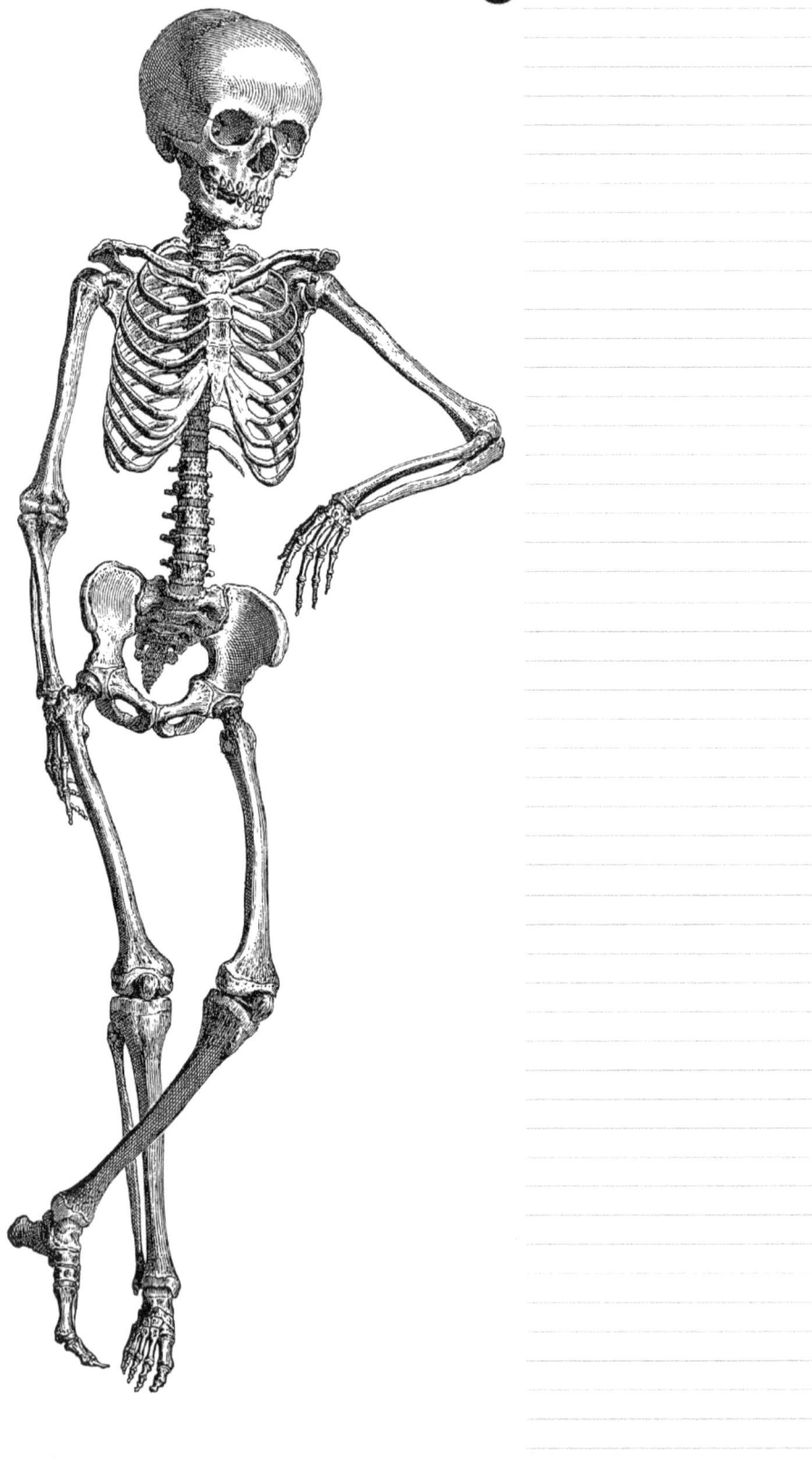

Plotting

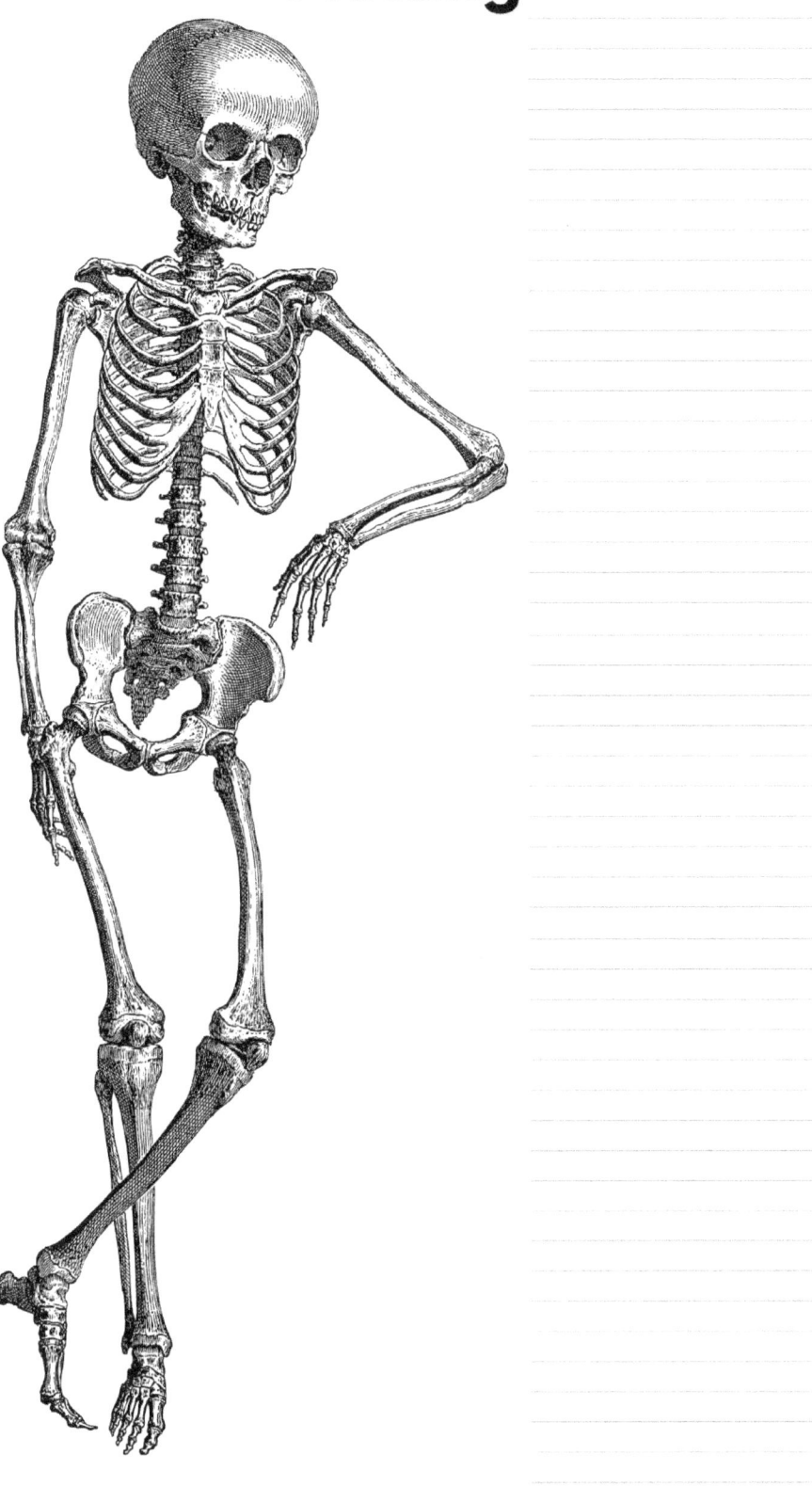

Plotting

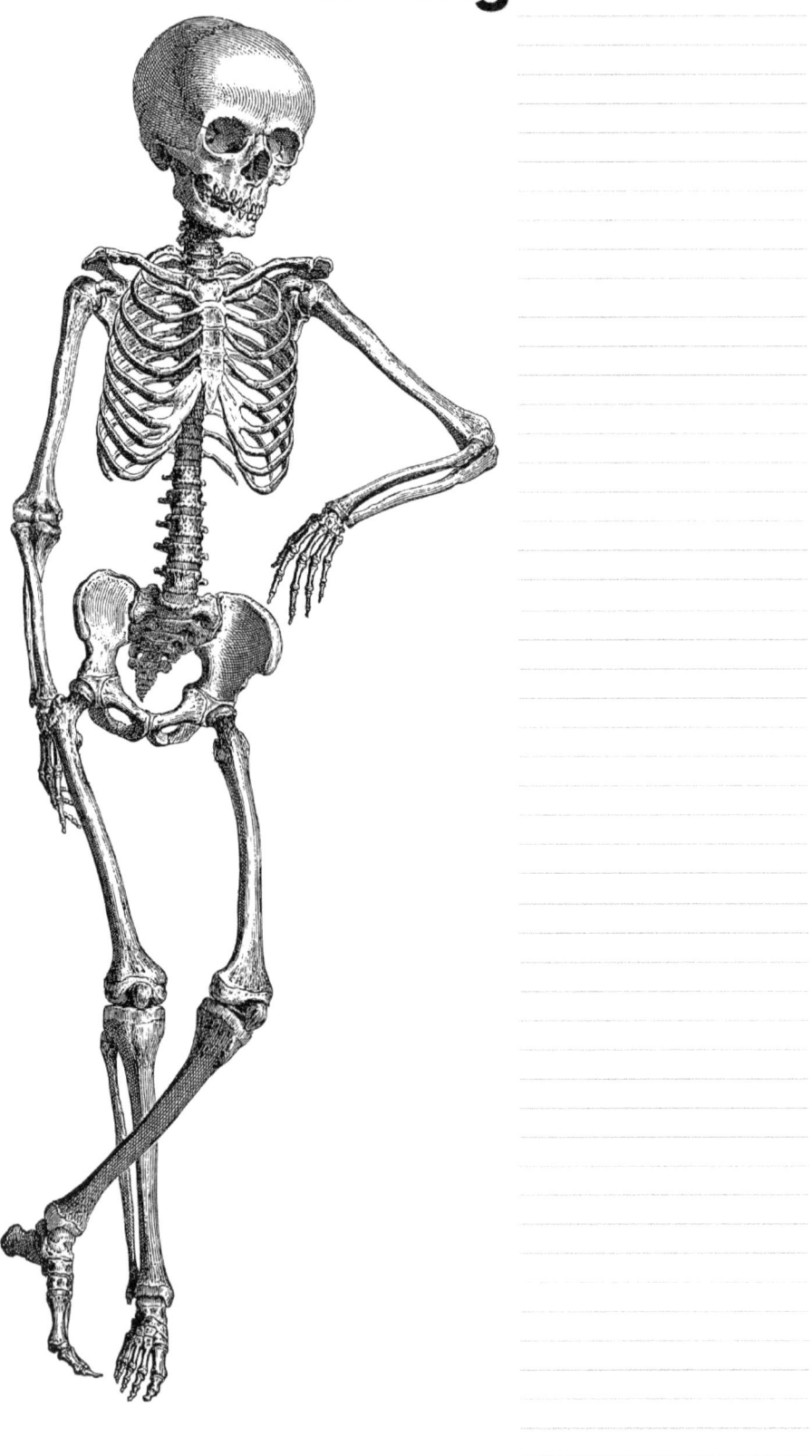

Progress Trackers

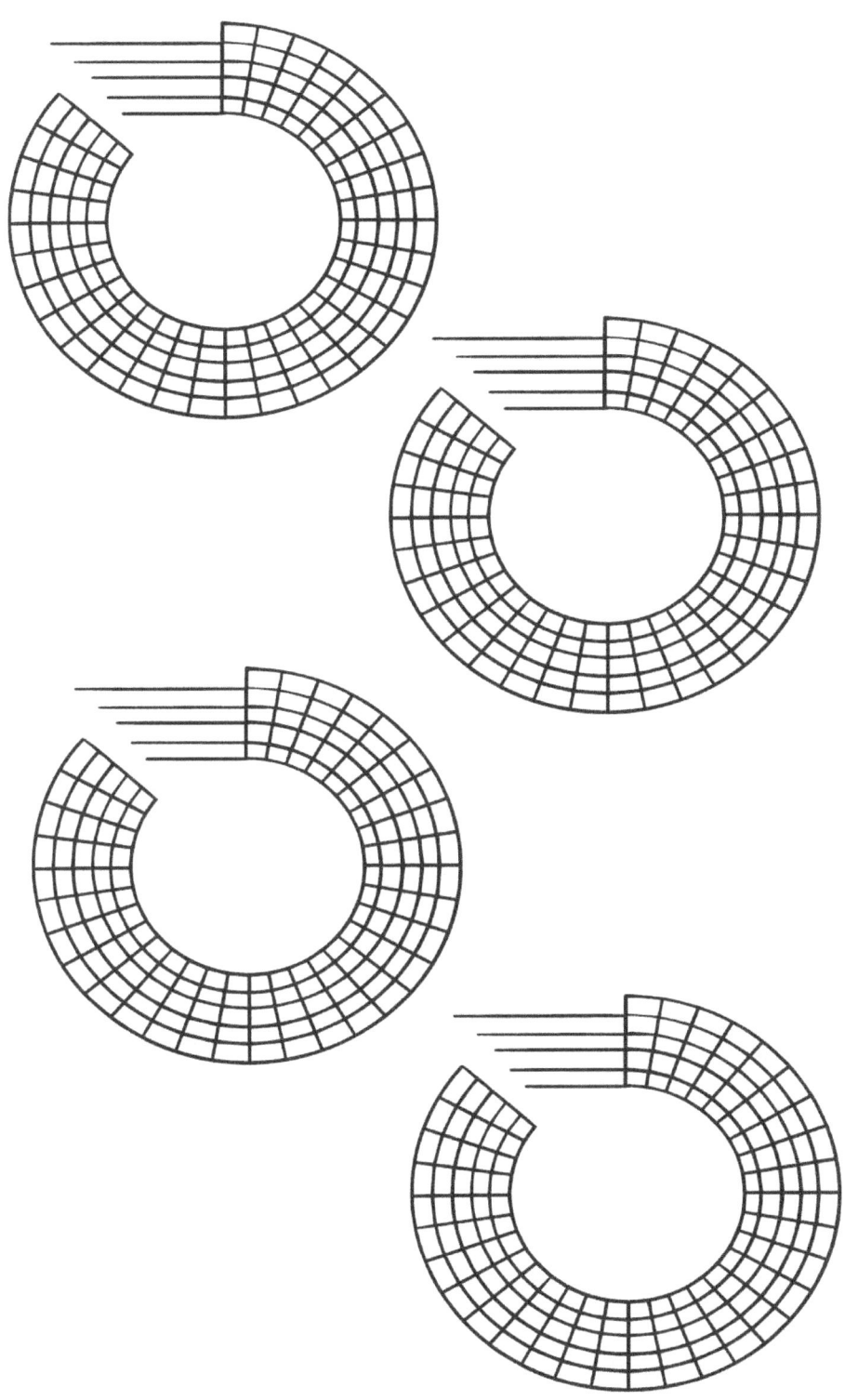

Progress Trackers

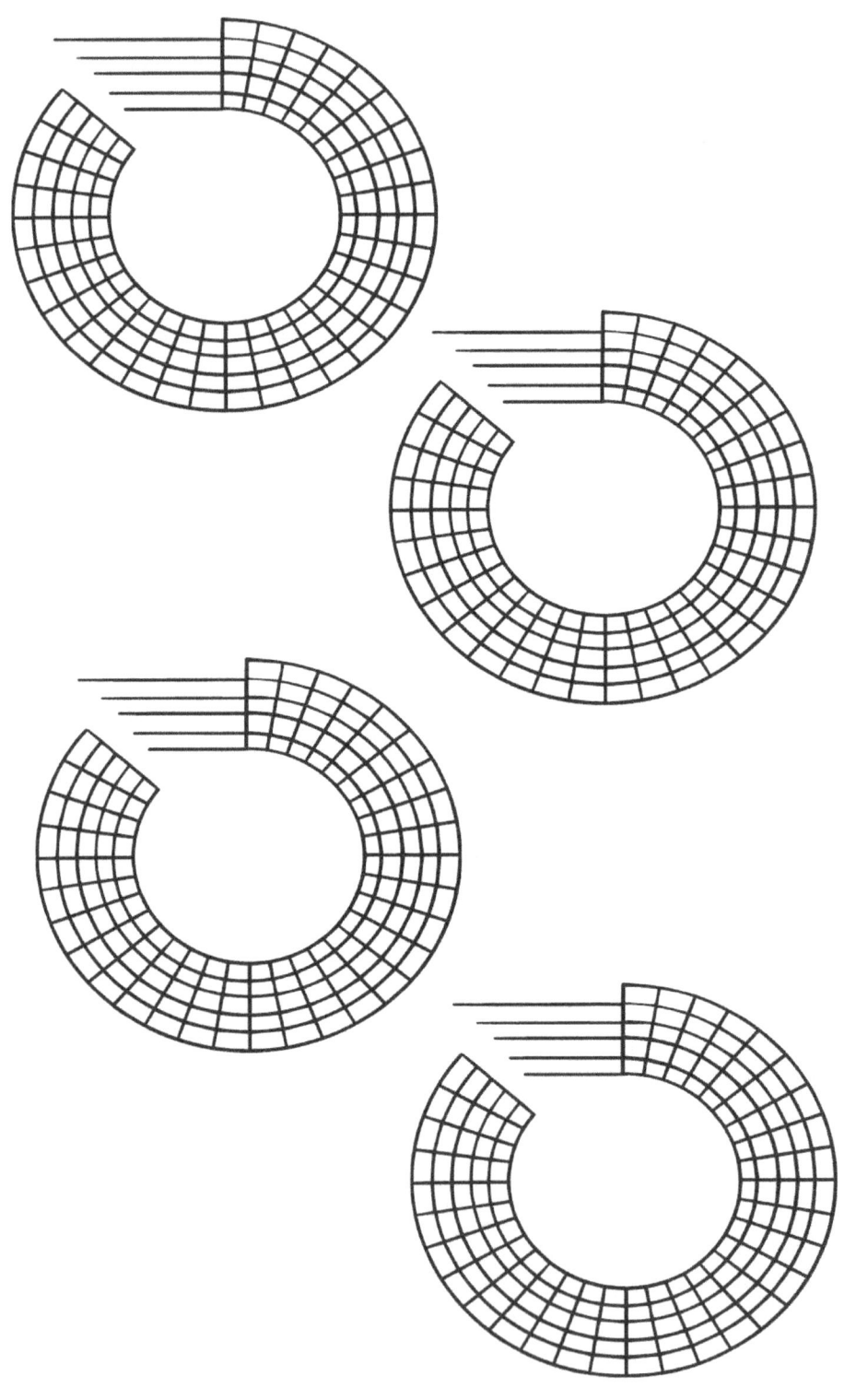

Progress Trackers

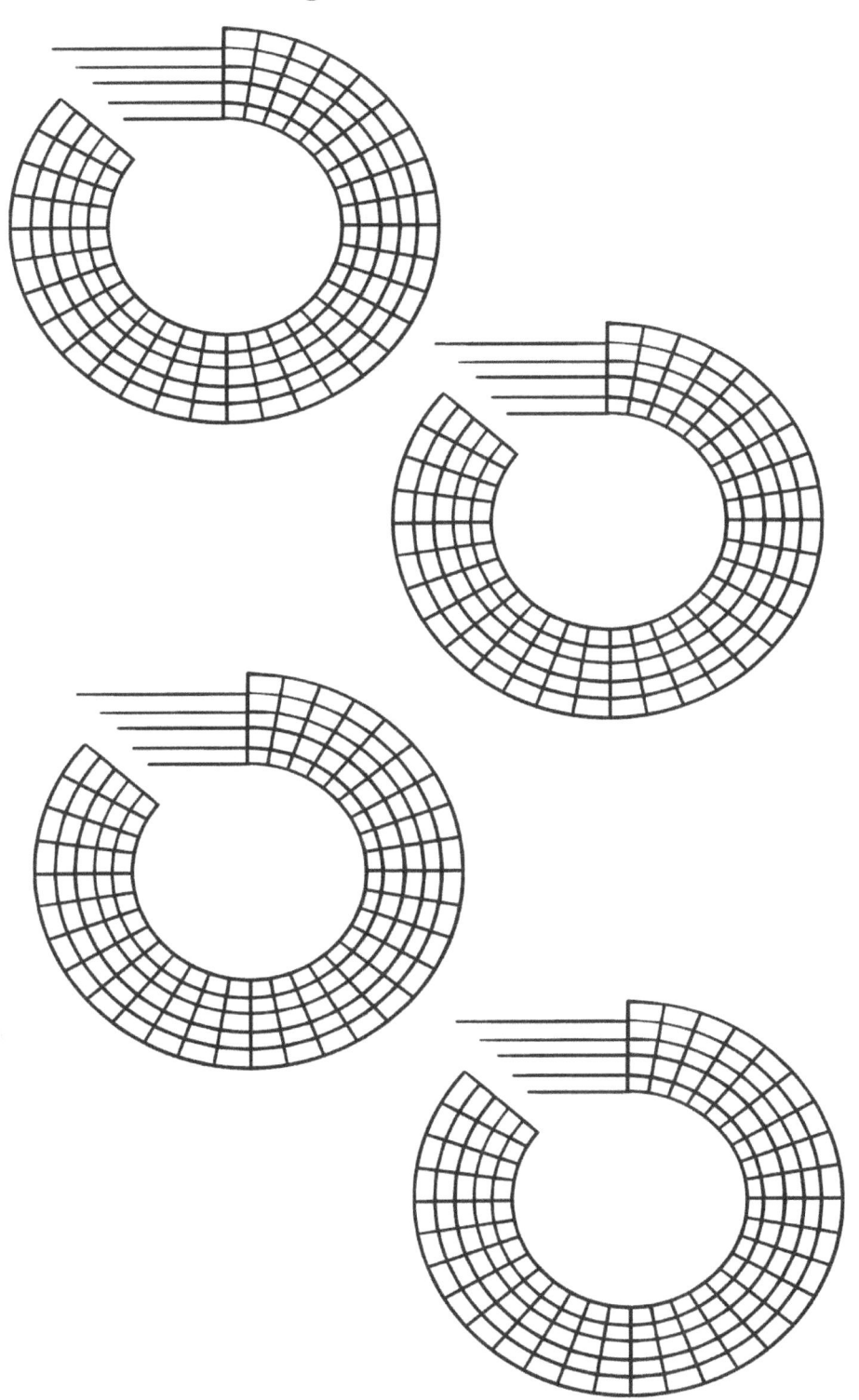

Progress Trackers

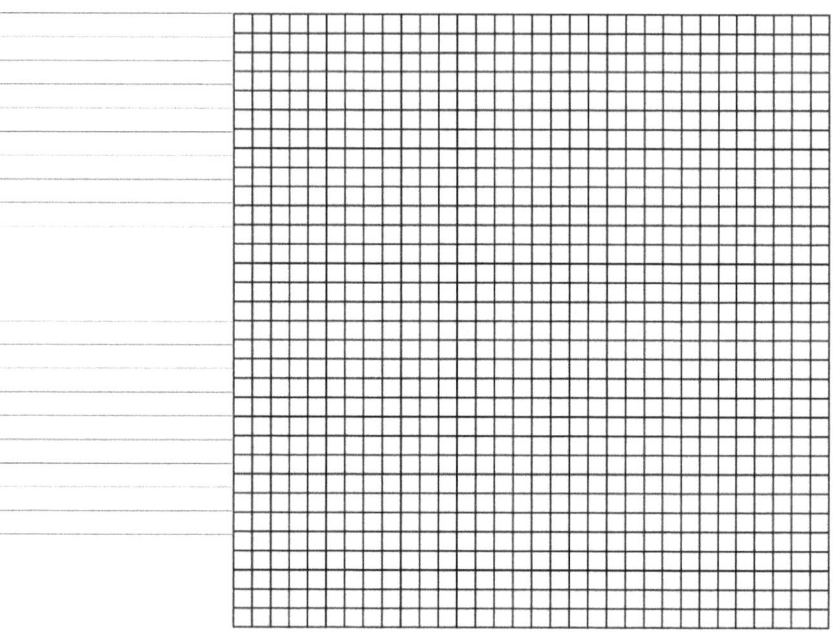

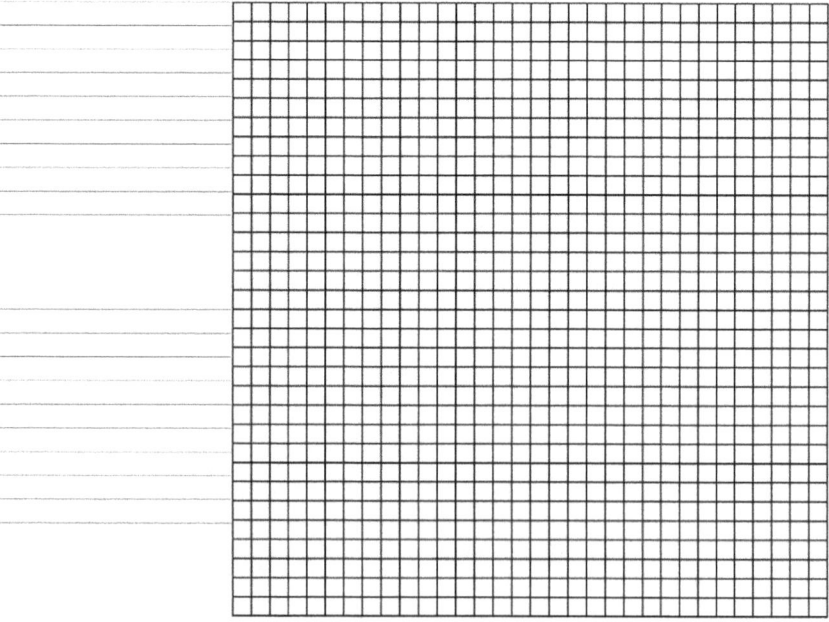

Progress Trackers

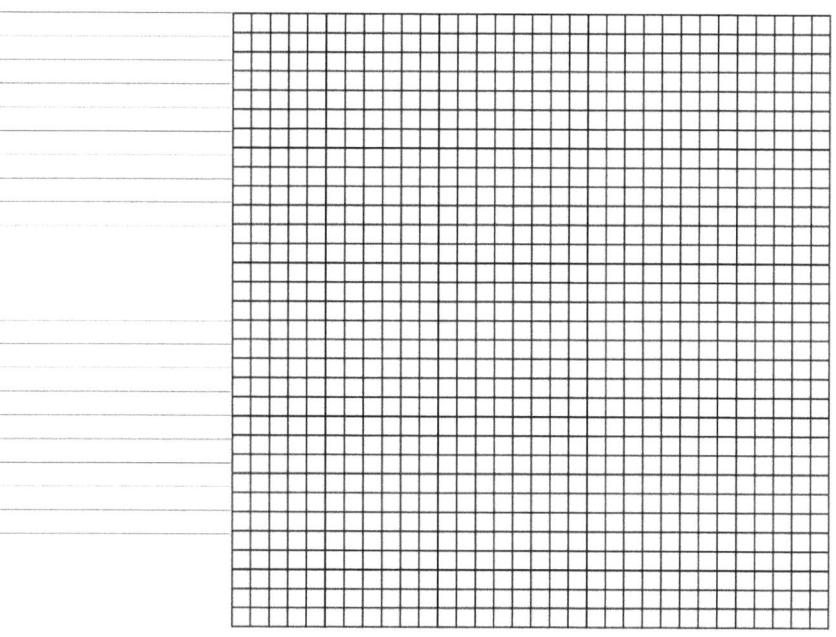

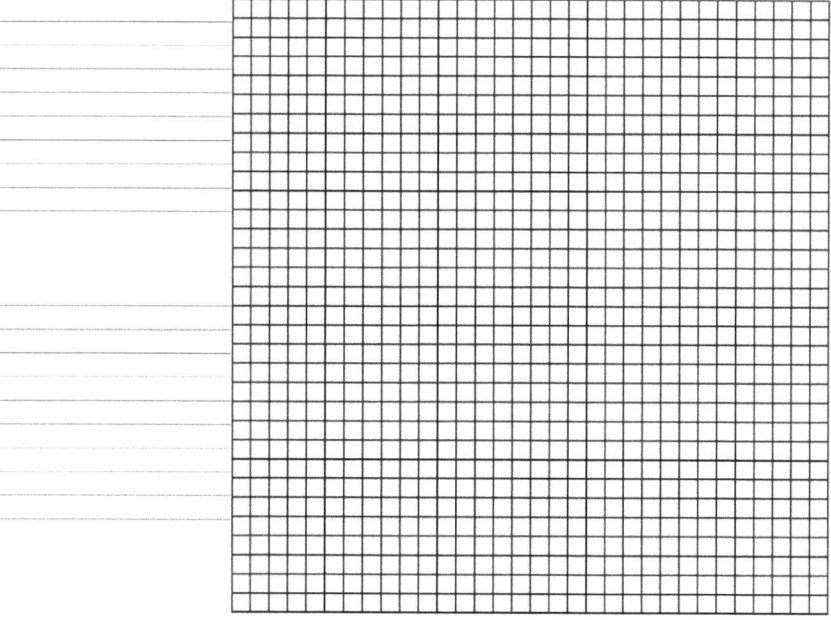

Progress Trackers

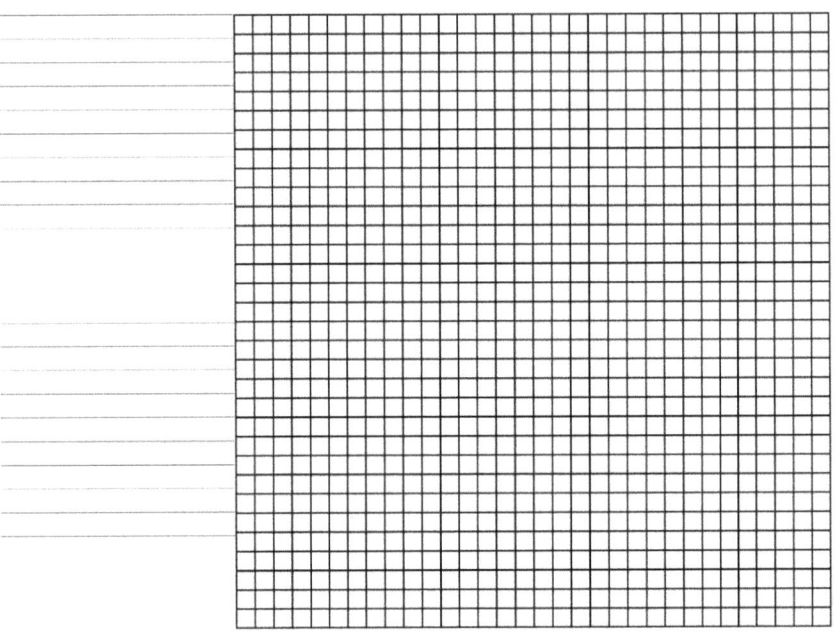

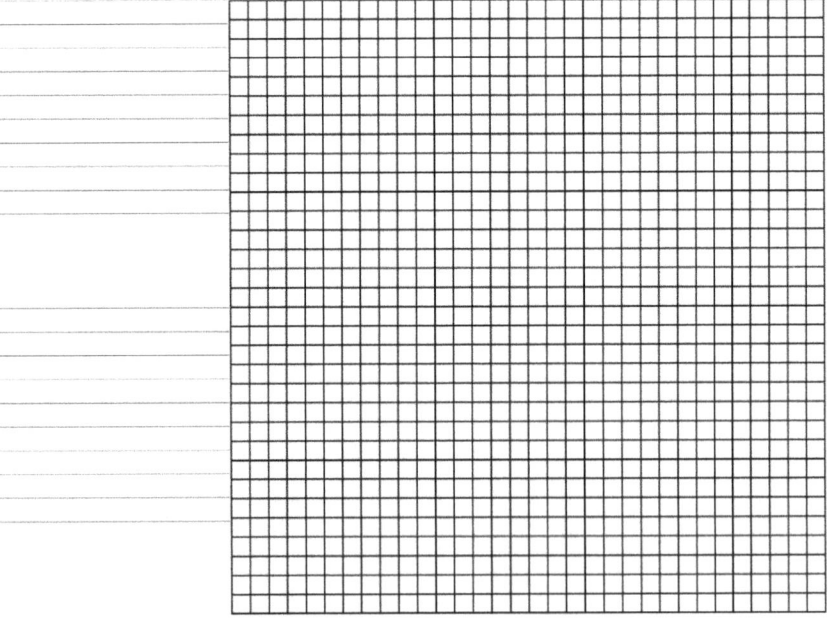